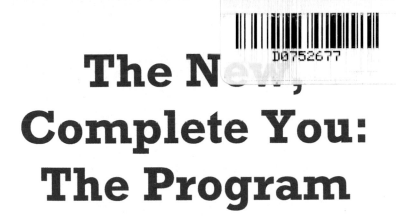

The New, Complete You: The Program

Transformation that Leads to a More Productive Life!

Justin R. Campbell

BK
ROYSTON
Publishing

BK Royston Publishing
P. O. Box 4321
Jeffersonville, IN 47131
502-802-5385
http://www.bkroystonpublishing.com
bkroystonpublishing@gmail.com

© Copyright – 2020

Cover Design: Elite Book Covers
Editor: Dr. Teresa Couts

ISBN-13: 978-1-951941-62-8

Printed in the United States of America

Dedication:

To every person who has yet to dream, has a dream, or desires to go further than the dream that has come true, this is for you. I know what it is like to have that dream since you were a kid, and I know what it is like for that dream to be fleshed out and matured to reality. There is a gift in you, this is why you cannot give up and this is why you cannot quit. Too many people are depending on you to make your dream come true. Whether your dream has come true or you are still working on it, keep building the inside (your characteristics), because this is what will prepare you and keep you when the dream comes true! Characteristics will keep you grounded and take you further than your gifts could ever do alone. I am proud of you. YES, YOU! I am proud of you for taking this journey and what it will do for your journey.

Table of Content

Introduction

As you go through this program, my hope is that all who participate will understand their character can continually be developed. The list I have provided in this program are not an exhaustive list of characteristics. However, I believe if you will learn and implement these characteristics into your life, you will be fruitful and prosperous, rather than unproductive and shortsighted.

What is the definition of character you ask? In so many words it is the distinctive traits and qualities that make up an individual's personality.

As you look at the table of contents, one through eight are the characteristics. Faith is the foundation all the other characteristics are built upon, and victory is what you are guaranteed to receive if you live by and heed to these characteristics. Please understand, I am not saying that if you have and institute these characteristics that you will never have any troubles or struggles. What I am saying, is if you implement, live by, and allow these characteristics to take root and become part of your personality, no matter what comes your way, you will be victorious because you will respond in a way that sees a solution above the problem!

For this program to be beneficial, you MUST complete it all. Do not rush through this program and allow it to lead you rather than for you to lead it. What I mean is, take as much time as is needed. Some sections may lend itself to more discussion than others. There may be a section that you need to go over a second time because it was that powerful. I recommend that you take full advantage of the reflection at the end of each characteristic. These traits are powerful! If done with a group, you should expect great conversation, as well as those participating to be emotional and breakthrough to occur. If you do this as a group, I recommend there being a make-up day for those who may miss a day. For those doing this program with a group, I would come up with an activity at the end of each day to help regulate group members emotions. If you do this by yourself, please give yourself enough time to think and respond to the questions, as well as to decompress and compose yourself once you are done.

I leave you with this: YOU WERE BORN AND ARE NECESSARY TO SOLVE A PROBLEM IN THIS WORLD! Allow these characteristics to take you to another level/dimension, no matter where you are in your journey. As long as there is breath in your body, you should continually be growing and fine-tuning your skills until the day you die. Knowledge is power; power is knowledge. If that knowledge never turns into wisdom, that power lies dormant! If you will be disciplined in learning and living out these characteristics, and learning others down the road, YOU WILL grow into the person you were always created and destined to be.

SECTION 1

FOUNDATION

Characteristic One: Faith

**Faith – confidence and complete belief or trust in a
person, concept, idea, or thing.**

First and foremost, you must distinguish between faith and
belief. Faith is not just believing. If you stop there, which
most of us do, you have barely scratched the surface. Faith
is believing in something AND obeying or following what
you say you believe. In addition, faith is more than just head
knowledge, but faith leads to action, whether doing or saying
something.

What is it that you have faith in and why? In the area you named,
has it led you to works (action; doing; accomplishment)?

_____

_____

_____

_____

_____

This is not math class, but let's look at an equation:
FAITH = BELIEF + CONFIDENCE + ACTION

**Belief – an opinion or judgement in which a person is
fully persuaded.**

This means your belief comes from being convinced of an
idea, concept, etc. This belief comes through acquiring
information or it can come through your experiences.

What are some experiences you have had in your life, that has shaped your current belief system?

_____

_____

_____

_____

_____

What information have you learned about yourself and/or been taught, that has shaped your current belief system?

_____

_____

_____

_____

_____

Understanding what belief is, means your beliefs can change over time as we gain more knowledge and experience more things throughout life. Let's remember that change does not always mean something negative. As you learn more, it may mean your current belief becomes even stronger. However, you could change your belief based on the new knowledge and experiences.

This brings us to a daunting fact: belief is a product of the mind. When a person has a victim mindset, they are already at a disadvantage when it comes to belief. Yet, even a person with a healthy mindset, will face trouble that can cause them to struggle with their belief.

Is there any belief you have that contradicts other beliefs, which keeps you from taking action?

_____
_____
_____
_____
_____

Sometimes we can get so caught up in the belief (knowledge, information, research) that all we have are words and manuscripts, but NO ACTION! That brings us to the other variable in this equation, confidence.

What is confidence to you?

_____
_____
_____
_____
_____

Do you really have confidence? How do you know you have or don't have confidence?

_____
_____
_____
_____
_____
_____
_____
_____
_____

Confidence – trust that is based on knowledge or past experience; belief that one can rely on someone or something.

Confidence is how firmly you hold to what you believe. One major barrier to confidence in what you believe, can be due to your lack of confidence in yourself. When you are not confident in your own abilities, this may make you question your ability in deciphering the information you receive. In other words, you second guess yourself. If this is you, do not fear. Confidence is not an innate, fixed characteristic. It's an ability that can be acquired and improved over time. The more confident you are, the more you will move forward with people and opportunities.

Tips to Confidence:
1. Build a confident mindset
2. Compare yourself kindly
3. Shake off self-doubt
4. Take safe risks
5. Do something just beyond your comfort zone
6. Don't be afraid to be wrong, and own up to your own mistakes
7. Do not put down other people/be humble
8. Able to ask for help
9. A good listener
10. Celebrate others

Conclusion:
When you believe the truth with enough confidence to take action, you exercise faith.

The question you must ask yourself is, "What is my truth?"

_____
_____
_____
_____
_____

What truth have you believed about yourself, your purpose, or your destiny that is a lie (meaning, you believe this is all you will ever be, when really you will be more, but you have based it off others false opinions)?

_____
_____
_____
_____
_____

I hope you can see how unbelief, which is believing things that aren't true (believing lies), completely clogs up the working of your faith. Unbelief prevents you from seeing, moving, and doing great and awesome things. STOP! REALLY, PAUSE AND GATHER YOURSELF FOR THIS NEXT PART.

Clear your mind for a second.

NOW, get that dream, initiative, or cause that you have always wanted to do in your mind. If you never have had one, think of one right now. PICTURE yourself fulfilling whatever it is you thought of (take as much time as you need here). The fact that you pictured it, means you saw it. Today, start to work your way backwards, know the truth, believe in that truth, and take action.

Who do you know or who can you ask, that can help you get to where you want to be (take the first step of ACTION)?

_____

_____

_____

_____

_____

Faith Reflection

SECTION 2

INWARD

Character Two: Virtue

Virtue (Moral Excellence) – has to do with your moral conduct and ethics in life. The key is it should be excellent, which means you should always be doing your best or being exceptionally good.

Let's start off with a question. Are you virtuous because it's what you deeply believe, or are you virtuous because you are afraid of the consequences or the repercussions?

_____

_____

_____

_____

_____

To possess a virtue is to be a specific kind of person with a certain complex mindset. A major aspect of this mindset is the wholehearted acceptance of a distinctive range of considerations as reasons for action. You must understand the order and importance of faith and virtue being the first two traits. Your virtues are going to be strongly impacted by what you believe and have confidence in. It is also good to mention here, that our soul consists of our mind, will, and emotions, which more specifically means our conscious and our subconscious. I mention this because your virtues form the soul with the habits that support moral behavior and control passions. Understanding this characteristic guides every other one. For if you understand and apply this one, every characteristic you learn after this, you will learn it for the right reason and use it with excellence.

Who is someone you can identify that has shown virtuous characteristics?

_____
_____
_____
_____
_____

How did their actions show this and how did their actions inspire you to develop that characteristic?

_____
_____
_____
_____
_____

You must ask yourself TODAY, "When a response is needed, is my nature one that is virtuous?" If you answer anything but yes, then you must get this characteristic before moving on. This is vital, because you must get to a place where you become a person of your word and actions, to the point it is second nature. It becomes second nature to do right, to be excellent, to be moral, and to ACT. A virtuous person will not be a spectator, but will be a person who acts on their morals and ethics. In other words, you must have guts to see through, to the end, what you believe.

What is something you believe in, that you know you could help or respond to, but have yet to do so? What is keeping you from moral excellence?

_____

_____

_____

_____

_____

For a second, I want you to think of how many opportunities you have missed or how many people you could have helped, had you acted on the virtues you believe in. In life, because you are worried about what others think and what others will say, you miss making the biggest impact on others lives. BUT TODAY, you are no longer living your life in fear or focused/worried on what others have to say. TODAY, you are going to take a step of faith and live, move, and walk, by the virtues you have and are developing through this program. And let me say this here. You will not always like the virtuous way, but you do it and are committed to it, because it is the excellent and right way or thing to do. When you act in this manner, is when you know you are truly living a virtuous life!

What areas of your life could you grow in moral excellence (attitudes, priorities, goals, purpose, at home, at work, at school, at church, etc.) and how?

_____

_____

_____

_____

_____

Conclusion:
Virtue or moral excellence will cause you to GO the extra mile. This characteristic will lead you to being committed to doing the right thing for others, which in return will bring your soul joy. When you operate in a virtuous way, you will give 110% without asking why or for who. You will have the attitude and disposition of I MUST because it is in my nature and character to be excellent based on my morals and beliefs. As you go through the rest of these characteristics, keep this one in the forefront of your mind, as it guides the next six.

> *"Moral excellence comes about as a result of habit. We become just by doing just acts, temperate by doing temperate acts, brave by doing brave acts."* *Aristotle*

How does this quote speak to you and challenge you in your quest of virtue or moral excellence? When answering this, think back to the sentence above about how habits form the soul, which then impact our conscious and subconscious.

_____
_____
_____
_____
_____

Virtue Reflection

_____

_____

_____

_____

_____

_____

_____

_____

_____

_____

_____

_____

_____

_____

_____

_____

_____

_____

_____

_____

_____

_____

_____

_____

_____

Character Three: Knowledge

Knowledge – understanding by way of studying or experience.

Without getting too deep, let me first clarify the subtle difference between information and knowledge.

Information, in short, is processed data about something or someone. And knowledge, to add a word to the above definition, is useful information gained through learning, studying, and experience. In our lives, we receive information of some sort and then filter out parts of that data.

From the filtered information, we take what we believe to be useful for that subject or whatever it is we are seeking information for, and we call that knowledge.

I hope you are continually seeing how these characteristics are flowing together and in order. Faith is the foundation, where you trust and are fully persuaded about a concept or idea. Then because you have virtue, you will take what you believe and use it in an excellent way. All of this is because you have received information and have translated it into knowledge!

What knowledge have you acquired to this point about yourself and your path?

_____

_____

_____

What further information or experiences do you need to acquire that will give you the knowledge to move one step closer to your dream or path?

_____

_____

_____

_____

_____

One word that is vital in the definition of knowledge is experience. This is what separates you from moving from good to great. I bet you know someone who knows all kind of information. Literally they know so much it makes you wonder, "Where did they acquire that and why do they even know that."

However, when you take a deeper look into the person's life, you realize all they have is information that has never been filtered, tried, or experienced to become knowledge.

This is why you must be intentional and purposeful about the experiences you choose. Everything you do has an effect on you one way or another. You also must be intentional and purposeful about what you read. As you do either of these, you are filtering out some kind of data, which then becomes your knowledge (good or bad, true or false).

Ask yourself this vital question: Am I where I am because I am operating off the wrong knowledge; because I am processing the wrong information? So, if you start today looking up the right information, you will then get the right knowledge. Will you make up in your mind to change directions, which will make your dreams come true and change your altitude (go higher)? Greater knowledge means great accountability. Once you know, there is now no excuses for not doing what you know.

Conclusion:
What I hope you take out of this section is that you can <u>know</u> what to do and where to go, if you filter through the right information. Knowledge is information that is broken down into action. Think of your brain as the map of knowledge. Data, information, and experiences are being stored there. From that knowledge, I then choose a course of action.

What direction might you need to re-evaluate or change due to the wrong knowledge you have been living from?

_____
_____
_____
_____
_____

Where has the information you have gathered been coming from: family experience, own experience, books, internet, school, magazines, TV, friends, work, etc.?

_____
_____
_____
_____
_____

Now that you will be intentional and purposeful, where will you get your information from?

_____
_____
_____
_____
_____

Knowledge Reflection

Character Four: Self-Control

Self-Control – to keep in check or control your own emotions, feelings and reactions. Controlling impulses, desires, and passions.

As you continue to grow, learn, add, and evaluate your characteristics; moral excellence (your exceptional moral ethics) guides every characteristic. Characteristic four through eight are more practical in nature than the first two, virtue and knowledge.

The website, verywellmind says, "Self-control is the ability to regulate and alter responses in order to avoid undesirable behaviors, increase desirable ones, and achieve long-term goals."

On a scale of 1 to 10, 1 being not at all and 10 being all the time, how well do you keep your emotions, feelings, and reactions in check?

Circle one below.

1   2   3   4   5   6   7   8   9   10

The key words, so far, are in check, control, regulate, and alter. I want you to understand now, emotions and feelings are real. We are all created with emotions, and it is unhealthy to try and not feel a certain way, even if negative. Do not miss that. To suppress the emotion, is to deny the facts. When you deny the facts, you do not deal with the emotion, therefore, a negative feeling occurs and you react in a way that is undesirable or impulsive. However, the goal is to identify the emotions and feelings, put them in check, and then react in a desirable way.

Before today, how have you understood your emotions or feelings?

_____

_____

_____

_____

_____

Do you believe feelings can be controlled? Why or why not?

_____

_____

_____

_____

_____

When you feel a way that is not to your liking, what do you do or how do you respond?

_____

_____

_____

_____

_____

It may help here to discuss what emotions and feelings are (see appendix A). In a sense, emotions are subconscious responses to certain external or internal events. For example, if there is a real threat, you do not have to ask yourself, "Am I afraid." There is no thinking involved. Internally, you feel it because your body responds with sweating, increased heartbeat, etc., and then that emotion brings a response of some sort. Feelings are subjective experiences of emotions and are driven by conscious thoughts and reflections.

Because of the emotion, I process that, whether true or false, and that process leads to a thought that becomes a feeling. You can have emotions without having feelings, however, you cannot have feelings without having emotions.

What I need you to understand is emotions help us to take action, survive, avoid danger, make decisions, and understand others. If you can control your emotions, your feelings will be appropriate, which will lead not only to the right behavior, but the right desires and passions. You have to understand this. Some emotions could be anger, fear, sadness, disgust, surprise, and happiness.

These emotions (and others), which are due to some external or internal event, can lead you to feelings of loneliness, confused, stressed, frustrated, excited, feeling safe or many other feelings.

What experiences, past or present, whether culturally, environmentally, or personally, have impacted your emotions?

_____
_____
_____
_____
_____

From your answer above, what feelings have occurred and what behaviors have followed due to those feelings?

_____
_____
_____
_____
_____

Conclusion:

If you are to exercise self-control, you must first learn to deal with your emotions and not suppress them. Then you must learn to keep your emotions in check and to regulate them. I hear you asking, "Well how do I do this?" First, take deep breaths. It sounds simple, but this can be challenging to do when the impulse to say something shoots up from the emotion that has been triggered. However, deep breaths slow down your thinking.

Secondly, develop some coping skills and find someone who can be a good outlet for you. Now that you have calmed your mind enough, not to respond to the emotion, you need to release the emotion by talking to someone, exercising, mindfulness, or some other healthy way.

Third, take the thought the emotion created, and replace it with a positive one. This is where the emotion now has created a feeling, and you must immediately replace it with an appropriate feeling.

Next, be selective about situations. We all know certain situations that trigger certain emotions. If it is within your control, avoid those, as to not trigger your own emotions.

Lastly, and one of the most important after deep breathing, is to forgive yourself for the emotions that may arise. When you forgive yourself, you then are able to detach from the negative feelings that could come, such as resentment and jealousy. As you forgive in this way, you stay in control and you do not relinquish your power over to your emotions.

What healthy activity or slogan can you implement through your day to ensure you keep your mind calm and at peace to help with your emotions?

_____

_____

_____

_____

_____

One thing I would suggest, along with what you answered above, is coming up with your own positive affirmation statement. For more assistance, google positive affirmation statements.

Self-Control Reflection

Character Five: Perseverance

Perseverance – staying the course regardless of difficulties. Being constant and steadfast in what you believe. This takes endurance, which means patiently waiting. Most things in life take time and commitment!

Let me say this now. Whether you come from a good home or a broken home, good parents, bad parents, foster parents, grandparents, or no parents, or a rich family or a poor family, there will be challenges, obstacles, and difficulties. And to be completely honest, sometimes these things are going to be called "LIFE." Yet, what I need you to know and believe, is regardless of life, people, or whatever has gone on, it has not canceled out your purpose. PLEASE, here me right now. Yes, you are hurting, it is painful, you have feelings that you need to let go and get under control, and you may have even given up on yourself, but your purpose in life is still intact and is waiting on you to walk in it. I hope that gave you some hope back.

Friedrich Nietzsche, observing those in concentration camps, said, *"He who has a why to live can bear almost any how."* Your 'why' serves as a constant motivator to keep you on track and persevering. If you have a reason or purpose, you can endure any misery. This does not mean you want it or it feels good, but you are able to persevere because you believe your why!

What is your why (why you do what you do)? What keeps you doing it day in and day out?

_____

_____

_____

_____

_____

What makes it important to you?

_____

_____

_____

_____

_____

"Many of life's failures are people who did not realize how close they were to success when they gave up." Thomas Edison

How does this quote speak to you and encourage you about something you may be going through now?

_____

_____

_____

_____

_____

To have perseverance, or any of these characteristics, is not based on a certain kind of person or a certain status. It is a grit that comes from within. It is a <u>healthy</u> stubbornness that will not quit, because you know this is your purpose and destination. So, the first thing I want to discuss about perseverance is staying the course and being consistent. This is where goals are vitally important. When you are goal-directed, in spite of what happens, you are able to stay the course, because you have the end in mind. Stephen Covey says, "To begin with the end in mind."

What are your goals for this month, this year, three years, and five years?

_____

_____

_____

_____

_____

Maybe you do not quite know your purpose or destination, so what are you passionate about? Basically, where are you going or headed?

_____

_____

_____

_____

_____

One thing that can detour you from staying the course is your own mindset. Have you ever started off persevering, but it just seems like the more you press forward, the harder you get knocked back? Then you start to think there is no use in continuing to try, and you would be better off staying where you are at, because you know how or are used to surviving in the mess you have been in. As the quote below says, you must not stop trying. At times, you must realize you are doing the best you can with what you have. Rather than look at all the bad or negative things, you must tell yourself, "I am worth it", "It will get better", "This is not happening to me, but for me", "I am an overcomer", and "No matter how long it takes, it will work out for me."

"A failure is not always a mistake. It may simply be the best one can do under the circumstances. The real mistake is to stop trying." B.F. Skinner

This is where faith must meet perseverance. The second line in the definition of perseverance says to be steadfast in what you believe. This is why knowing and being confident in what you believe is vital to these characteristics. When you are steadfast, this means nothing or no one can move you off the course of your life. I know that person lied on you, or they stole your idea or creation, or you financially needed that yes, but got a no, or you are tired and weary, or you have tried everything and do not see how it will work. But as the quote below says, do not let any of this make you believe a single failure of defeat is the final defeat.

"Never confuse a single defeat with a final defeat." F. Scott Fitzgerald

Let's dig in here. When you know that plan or dream is for you or even if you do not know, when challenges arise, what makes you give up or stop trying?

_____
_____
_____
_____
_____

I mentioned above that you can learn to survive in your mess, rather than change. A lot of times, this is due to not just being afraid of the unknown, but being afraid of success.

How do you persevere through feelings of success and fears or others that arise in these kind of situations?

_____

_____

_____

_____

_____

> *"Perseverance is the hard work you do after you get tired of doing the hard work you already did."* *Newt Gingrich*

You must know that as you persevere, it will take time and commitment. The quote above says it all. When you get tired of doing the hard work, you keep doing the hard work you already did. This comes from a true and deep desire to succeed. See, sometimes you do not realize that your desire is weak, until you fall and give up, or you see others succeeding.

At this point, you realize your desire for that goal or purpose must increase. I can tell you from personal experience, and I hope this pushes and encourages you today, there is nothing like working hard and finally getting to the goal you desired and set out for yourself. As Thomas Edison said above, so many of you are close to success, but you gave up right before achieving your goal or dream.

Conclusion:
What I hope you take out of this, is you must have perseverance to be victorious. Whether difficulties, hurdles, or just life, you are going to have to endure and be committed to what you believe in. This is why you must have faith and then build upon that faith. When you have a strong faith, and build perseverance upon that faith, you may have a situation

or event of failure in your life, but you will be able to say to yourself, "I failed, however, I am not a failure." Once you have done this, you will no longer be worried if your dream or goal will come true, but will be committed and steadfast to your why and persevere till the end, because you know it will happen.

I used to tell my students at New Albany High School (in Indiana) all the time, "They were born and are necessary to solve a problem" (a paraphrase from Myles Munroe). I need you and the world needs you to patiently endure and stay the course regardless of the difficulties that will arise. For when you persevere, greatness will be realized. Perseverance is the characteristic that will get you from potential to activation.

What habit can you start or reinitiate, that can help you persevere toward your purpose?

_____
_____
_____
_____
_____
_____
_____
_____
_____
_____

Perseverance Reflection

Perseverance Reflection

_____

_____

_____

_____

_____

_____

_____

_____

_____

_____

_____

_____

_____

_____

_____

_____

_____

_____

_____

_____

_____

_____

_____

_____

_____

_____

_____

_____

_____

_____

SECTION 3

UPWARD

Character Six: Piety

Piety – one part of this definition is a behavior that is morally correct. Think about this, as the characteristic that helps you to uphold justice, do what is right, and gives you the desire to live out what you believe. Also you can think about piety as being reverent and done for the benefit of others or with the intention of encouraging good (pious).

A good question to start off with is explain how your moral compass is?

_____

_____

_____

_____

_____

Are you easily persuaded to do wrong and go against your morals to fit in? If so, why?

_____

_____

_____

_____

_____

"For though we love both the truth and our friends, piety requires us to honor the truth first." Aristotle

This characteristic gets down to the heart of the matter: what helps you do right or good? Are you only being moral to uphold a high self-image? Are you only doing right because you are too afraid of consequences? Or are you behaving morally because this is who you are and because of the many characteristics we have already looked at are in you? I will give you some room to jot down some thoughts from these questions.

_____
_____
_____
_____
_____
_____
_____
_____
_____
_____

True piety is done with the right heart. True piety does not seek to do right to earn a reward or recognition, but seeks to do right because it is the only option. I hear you saying, "Justin, I have a choice." My response to your statement is in our heart there should not be room for a choice in this circumstance. You must have your mind made up when you wake up every morning that you are going to walk out your beliefs to the best of your ability, even if it makes you unpopular with others.

If you sometimes find yourself needing recognition or needing to make a scene when you do something for another, why? Where does this need come from?

_____
_____
_____
_____
_____
_____
_____
_____
_____
_____

What should give you pure joy is the smile on the person's face you just helped. Better yet, simply that you followed your heart and did the right thing. Because unfortunately, everyone will not respond with a smile or a thank you, even when you do a moral or good thing.

Too many times, you can allow the other person's response to dictate if you did the right thing. Part of this comes from your own preconceived expectations which are not met by their response. This is why you must want to do right and not base it on anything except the fact you can lay your head down at night knowing you were honest to who you are.

"Always be a first-rate version of yourself and not a second-rate version of someone else." Judy Garland

Conclusion:

As you are nearing the end of these characteristics, piety is asking you TODAY, will you live out what you have faith in. Piety does not allow you to just say I have these characteristics. Piety shines a spotlight on you and puts you on the witness stand, to hold you accountable for what you say you possess. Will you be perfect, no. But you can be intentional about walking out what you say you believe and doing what is right. As you do what is morally right and what is just, not only will your heart be filled with joy and peace, you will be the change the world needs!

Piety Reflection

SECTION 4

OUTWARD

Character Seven:
Brotherly Kindness

Brotherly Kindness – love for one another. Like what you would (should) have with your own flesh and blood.

This is a stubborn love that shows a person love as if they are your brother or sister because **you** care. It has nothing to do with what they have done or paying them back. It's just in you and you do it. Brotherly kindness starts with evaluating some of your own values. These values are selfishness, humility, charitable, and selflessness.

As we start this characteristic, write about how these four values reflect you. As you write about these, try to connect how you got to the value. Was it due to what you saw or were you taught to act that way?

_____
_____
_____
_____
_____

Read these two quotes:

> *"Show respect even to people who don't deserve it, not as a reflection of their character, but as a reflection of yours."*
> *Dave Willis*

"Respect for ourselves guides our morals; respect for others guides our manners."
Laurence Sterne

How do these two quotes speak to you about respect? Do you believe what they say? Why or why not?

_____

_____

_____

_____

_____

_____

_____

When you have brotherly kindness, you have love and respect for others. Respect is very hard for many people. Many believe respect is earned. Many believe if you do not give respect, then you do not get respect. I take a different stance on this. If I were to ask you, "Are you respectful," most people would say, "Yes!" If you are respectful, then this means it is a characteristic that is in you. Therefore, I am not respecting you because you deserve it, just as I am not treating you in a loving way because you deserve it. I am respecting you, because I am a respectful person and my respecting you is not going to change based on how you treat me. This is hard for some, because rather than seeing the strength in being respectful or loving, they see it as a weakness and being walked over.

The golden rule says you should treat others as you would want to be treated, NO EXCEPTIONS. Yes, culture and knowing your history is very important and should not be forgotten or overlooked. However, that should not lead to a conceited attitude of better than or of ostracizing another group, but it should bring us together to appreciate and learn from each other. As it has been said, we are all human and we all bleed red. The question for you today, is will you learn and appreciate those differences, and not allow them to create fear in you, but still love the person because it is what is in their heart that matters?

Think about a person you do not like or do not get along with. Where did your disdain for them come from? Is it because of what you heard about them from someone else? Is it because your family or friends did not like the person so you chose not to like them as well? Did you ever give the person a chance, or did you choose to dislike them because of some prejudice or discrimination?

_____

_____

_____

_____

_____

_____

_____

_____

_____

_____

_____

Let me give a little example here. I think about gangs. Regardless of why people join gangs, once they join, they have to follow and abide by the rules and beliefs of that gang. If a person is affiliated with the gang, and they believe the gang has their best interest at hand, people set aside all of their beliefs, and take on the beliefs of that gang, even if they do not agree. How many times do we judge a particular group, simply because we take on the misconceptions (wrong beliefs) of someone else, the majority, or the culture, rather than seeing the person as just that, A PERSON OR HUMAN BEING!

Now, let me say here, I am not saying, do not see the differences. It is okay to see color (race), because within this is history, culture, and other things. What I am saying is as you see the differences, get to know the individual. Do not let others and society make you stereotype a person or group of people.

After thinking about what has been said, rate yourself on showing brotherly kindness. 0 being I do not show this to all and 10 being I freely show this to all.

1   2   3   4   5   6   7   8   9   10

Conclusion:
Brotherly kindness shows itself with bearing with others, sacrificing your needs for another, warning others when they are doing wrong or to keep them from harming themselves, lifting others up, which when you do, in return you are lifted up, and doing all you can to make and keep peace.

You yearn for connection. But your own prejudices and ignorance blocks you from receiving that connection to the fullest extent, as well as keeps you from helping others. Think about how you felt when you did the simplest thing for someone else. It may have been holding the door open for someone, helping someone pick something up they dropped, paying for someone's meal, buying a gift for someone just because, or helping someone that was alone or being talked about. When you show love, it warms your heart, regardless of if you know the person or not. Make up in your heart and mind, that you will be selfless and charitable to love another, based simply on the fact you have brotherly kindness residing in you!

Brotherly Kindness Reflection

Character Eight: Love

Love – being selfless. Doing charitable deeds or acts for others. Giving a gift out of pure love, just because.

I have to start off with a question here. Explain how you feel about giving something you love away to someone else? Is this easy or challenging for you and why?

_____
_____
_____
_____
_____
_____
_____
_____

You started with the characteristic of faith and you are finishing with love. Love is vital to life. I believe you can better show true love, as you mature in the characteristics above. Love is in you, but I believe love gets tainted due to experiences you go through, thereby, causing you to show love in a negative way.

First and foremost, you must love yourself. A word that can be used when talking about love is benevolence. You must not only have good will toward others, but yourself as well. Good will is seen in friendliness, compassion, kindness, and generosity. As you are able to be benevolent to yourself, you are more able to be benevolent to others.

I know this will be tough, but what challenges do you see in loving yourself?

_____

_____

_____

_____

_____

_____

_____

_____

Why is it easier for you to love someone else rather than yourself?

_____

_____

_____

_____

Many times, you show more compassion and love to others, because you do not want to deal with your own issues. You also are more loving to others than yourself, because it gives you a sense of achievement. But here is what I really want you to hear today. At the end of the day, you cannot fake yourself out when you are alone or when you lay your head down at night. Also, know that you will be able to do more for that person as you have a better understanding of yourself. When your needs are met for yourself, it enables you to think more clearly and respond more effectively.

When you show goodwill, it will increase your inner happiness and peace. So many times, we base our inner peace on wishing situations and life's challenges will change. However, you have the power within yourself to impact your mindset, regardless of what is going on. Being selfless means, you are being and exercising the characteristics you have previously gone through. It is hard to have peace, when you are being someone else or treating someone else differently than what you believe.

How have you seen this inner battle within yourself, where you felt bad or guilty for treating someone a certain way than what you know you should have?

_____
_____
_____
_____
_____
_____
_____
_____

Selfless love is tough, because you choose to love someone based on what is best for them and not based on what you want. Now let me say this here, this does not mean staying in a relationship that is wrong. I must say this, because if a person is verbally, physically, or emotionally abusing you, this is toxic and you must be selfless and love you and leave. Selfless love may cause you to sacrifice, but better worded, it should be compromise. Selfless love is not judgmental. This means you may confront someone if they are hurting themselves, but you do not judge why their behavior is why it is, you just help. Selfless love requires a listening spirit. Not assuming, but listening.

As you reread over some of the examples above, how well do you show this kind of selfless love? How can you do better, even if you are doing good?

_____
_____
_____
_____
_____

Conclusion:

If you want to love yourself better, as well as others, you must be okay with the fact no one is perfect. It is good to strive for perfection and to set goals realistically and high, but know if you come short, it does not mean the person or you are a failure.

As you continue to show yourself benevolence and goodwill, it will become much easier for you to show others goodwill and even get to a place of forgiveness. As you are showing selfless love, you inevitably learn and become more empathetic. When you are empathetic, you are able to put yourself in someone else's shoes. This allows you to treat people based on your characteristics and not based on how they are or what they are doing. Let love radiate from your heart, and then watch your heart be filled with warmth, joy, and peace!

> *"Selfless love is always costly; fear can't afford it, pride doesn't understand it and friends never forget it."* Bob Goff

> *"He who nurtures benevolence for all creatures within his heart overcomes all difficulties and will be the recipient of all types of riches at every step."* Chanakya

SECTION 5

CULMINATION

New Mindset: Victory

Victory – success over an opponent or opposition. Specifically, this win is the victory or success over self!

By following these characteristics, you are guaranteed to be complete, which equals victory!

The fact you are victorious now means that from your fruitfulness (what you have added, benefited from, or grown due to these characteristics), you will be able to continually plant seeds that will sprout in others and cause them to be productive!

Now that you are at the end, I am so excited for how these characteristics will help you become a better version of yourself. Of course, these characteristics are not the only list, but to know and possess these is a major start. I am proud of you for not just starting, but finishing. I am proud of you because you put in the work to answer some challenging questions so RIGHT NOW, you can walk in victory. You should celebrate right now with a scream, a dance, and a big hug to yourself.

As I finish this, I am already dancing and shouting for you, because I know you are a stronger individual and that will lead to others being the beneficiary of your greatness.

So many times you realize and know the battle is within yourself. You know how it feels to negotiate with your own mind, only to lose and still not accomplish what you wanted. You know what it is like to feel guilty after doing something you did not want to and how it feels to blame others and make excuses, when really you are the culprit. BUT THAT IS OVER WITH NOW! Say it with me: THE OLD SELF IS DONE, THE MORE PRODUCTIVE SELF IS HERE! Will you fall short, yes. But when you fall short now, you will spring back up like the kids inflatable punching bag.

Since you know you are victorious, now is the time to relook at where you are at in life. Take this time to look at your goals and where you are going. Evaluate the people you have with you and around you. Set SMART goals for the next month, year, and 3 years (appendix B). Take serious the information you read and watch. Because you realize who you are on the inside, do not be scared or afraid to make those changes, because the hardest change has been made in your heart. Keep being victorious and always work from the inside out.

Here is your last homework assignment. I want you to create for yourself an affirmation statement. This is a statement that is positive and defines and encompasses all of what you stand for as well as where you are going. It should be one to three sentences and this is something you should say every morning and whenever you need a reminder.

_____

_____

_____

_____

_____

_____

_____

For example, I will give you mine: I will love God by my actions, watching what I say, teaching others, reading His word, saying Yes to His will and living at the level God has called me to live. I will increase in wisdom and discernment to obey and walk in the will of God.

For me, this leads and guides me. When I say this statement, it reminds me of whose I am and who will help me get to where I am going. Again, this is just an example for me. Now you create your own and thanks for taking this journey.

PLEASE RECOMMEND THIS TO OTHERS, SO THEY TOO CAN BE VICTORIOUS AND MORE PRODUCTIVE.!

P.S. A great resource and compliment to this program is my book "The New, Complete You Life Between The Lines."

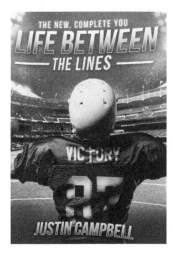

Appendix A:

In the center are the emotions. The next two layers are feelings.

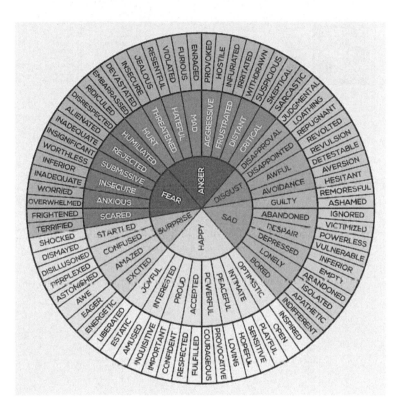

At the top are emotions. In the boxes are the feelings based on the level of intensity.

Intensity of Feelings	HAPPY	SAD	ANGRY	AFRAID	ASHAMED
HIGH	Elated Excited Overjoyed Thrilled Exuberant Ecstatic Fired up Passionate	Depressed Agonized Alone Hurt Dejected Hopeless Sorrowful Miserable	Furious Enraged Outraged Boiling Irate Seething Loathsome Betrayed	Terrified Horrified Scared stiff Petrified Fearful Panicky Frantic Shocked	Sorrowful Remorseful Defamed Worthless Disgraced Dishonored Mortified Admonished
MEDIUM	Cheerful Gratified Good Relieved Satisfied Glowing	Heartbroken Somber Lost Distressed Let down Melancholy	Upset Mad Defended Frustrated Agitated Disgusted	Apprehensive Frightened Threatened Insecure Uneasy Intimidated	Apologetic Unworthy Sneaky Guilty Embarrassed Secretive
LOW	Glad Contented Pleasant Tender Pleased Mellow	Unhappy Moody Blue Upset Disappointed Dissatisfied	Perturbed Annoyed Uptight Resistant Irritated Touchy	Cautious Nervous Worried Timid Unsure Anxious	Bashful Ridiculous Regretful Uncomfortable Pitied Silly

The five core emotions run left to right across the top of the table. Manifestations of each emotion based upon the intensity felt are described down each of the columns in the table.

ACTION PLAN

Room: _____   Time Period: _____

OBJECTIVES (List of Goals)	TASKS (what you need to do to achieve the goals)	SUCCESS CRITERIA (how you will identify your success)	TIME FRAME (by when you need to complete the tasks)	RESOURCES (what or who can help you complete tasks)

BELLA

References:

1. Cherry, Kendra. "How to Improve Your Self-Control." *Verywell Mind*, 6 Apr. 2020, www.verywellmind.com/psychology-of-self-control-4177125.

2. S, Surbhi, et al. "Difference Between Information and Knowledge (with Comparison Chart)." *Key Differences*, 20 Jan. 2018, keydifferences.com/difference-between-information-and-knowledge.html.

3. *The Free Dictionary*, Farlex, www.thefreedictionary.com/dictionary.htm.

4. Mama, Betsy at Zen, et al. "What's The Difference Between Feelings And Emotions?" *The Best Brain Possible*, 23 Apr. 2019, thebestbrainpossible.com/whats-the-difference-between-feelings-and-emotions/.

About Author

Justin Campbell is a devoted man of God who understands he is just an earthen vessel being used by God. Justin is the owner of M.I.G.H.T. LLC, Men/Women In God's Hands Transformed. Through M.I.G.H.T. his mission is to encourage people to walk fully in their purpose through positivity, creative solutions, and self-empowerment. Justin is a member of Canaan Christian Church in Louisville, KY where he is a bible study teacher on Sunday mornings, over the prayer ministry, and is a Mental Health Therapist.

Justin has been called on by churches, schools, and others to speak to youth and adults. "I love being able to allow God to use me to be a blessing to those in attendance, because I know it is appointed by God and someone will be blessed!" God has also gifted Justin to start a Facebook group called "Moving Past your Past, to Life and Joy" where he posts encouraging videos.

At the end of the day, Justin just wants to be used so that God is glorified. He spends much time in the word of God, in prayer, reading Christian books, and listens to podcasts on marketing, entrepreneurship, and leadership. He is not perfect by any means, but he understands, like Paul, he is what he is by the grace of God and all his labor is due to the grace of God that worketh in him!

If you are looking for an inspiring life speaker, emcee, or a therapist, please connect with Justin at his website below. You can also purchase his book, a t-shirt, and see clips of his talks on his website as well. Join Justin on all his social media platforms (Facebook, Instagram, YouTube, Twitter, and LinkedIn) by searching mightllc.

Website: www.mightllc.com

"To be yourself in a world that is constantly trying to make you something else is the greatest accomplishment."

— **Ralph Waldo Emerson**

"You may not control all the events that happen to you, but you can decide not to be reduced by them."

— **Maya Angelou, Letter to My Daughter**

Justin R. Campbell, Owner

Made in the USA
Middletown, DE
14 October 2021